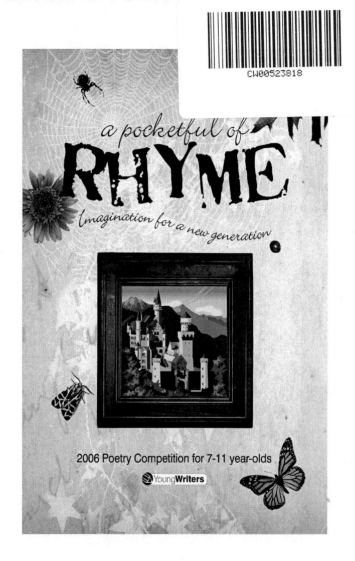

a pocketful of
RHYME

Imagination for a new generation

2006 Poetry Competition for 7-11 year-olds

YoungWriters

Eastern Rhymes
Edited by Claire Tupholme

 Young**Writers**

First published in Great Britain in 2007 by:
Young Writers
Remus House
Coltsfoot Drive
Peterborough
PE2 9JX
Telephone: 01733 890066
Website: www.youngwriters.co.uk

SB ISBN 1 84602 718 7

Foreword

Young Writers was established in 1991 and has been passionately devoted to the promotion of reading and writing in children and young adults ever since. The quest continues today. Young Writers remains as committed to the nurturing of poetic and literary talent as ever.

This year's Young Writers competition has proven as vibrant and dynamic as ever and we are delighted to present a showcase of the best poetry from across the UK and in some cases overseas. Each poem has been selected from a wealth of *A Pocketful Of Rhyme* entries before ultimately being published in this, our fourteenth primary school poetry series.

Once again, we have been supremely impressed by the overall quality of the entries we have received. The imagination, energy and creativity which has gone into each young writer's entry made choosing the poems a challenging and often difficult but ultimately hugely rewarding task - the general high standard of the work submitted ensured this opportunity to bring their poetry to a larger appreciative audience.

We sincerely hope you are pleased with this final collection and that you will enjoy *A Pocketful Of Rhyme Eastern Rhymes* for many years to come.

Contents

Emily Bird (10)   35
Victoria Penhale (9)   36
Eleanor Taylor   37
Mikey Sharman-Gutteridge (10)   38
April Coyle (10)   39
Brogan Carpenter (11)   40
Joshua Croxford   41
Annabelle Penhale (9)   42
Zara Hale (10)   43

Clare Middle School, Clare

Saskia Caddock (9)   44
Amelia Dzioba (9)   45
Emily Goodwin (9)   46
Cydney Nunn (9)   47
Charlotte Bareham (9)   48
Rhianna Dourado (9)   49
Eleanor Rodwell-Cullup (10)   50
James Curran (9)   51
Max Murphy (10)   52
Emily-Ann Caton (9)   53
Sam Ager (9)   54
Adam Chinery (10)   55
Autumn Wulff (10)   56
Claire Morey (10)   57
Harriet Potter (9)   58
Billy Guiry (9)   59
Ben Rawlings (9)   60
Elspeth Walker (9)   61
Paige Mylchreest (9)   62
Ellen Beattie (9)   63
Marcus Brooker (10)   64

Great Casterton CE Primary School, Great Casterton

Madeleine Warnes (9)   65
Aimee West (9)   66
Melissa Eddisford (9)   67
Charlie Parker & Jodie Hunt (9)   68
Jack Woodhouse & Thomas Watterson (9)   69
Hollie Raeburn (11)   70
Ellen Roke (9)   71

Jessica Harrison (9)   72
Laura Hartshorne (10)   73
Francesca Cooper (9)   74
Larna Thorpe (9)   75

Old Buckenham Community Primary School, Old Buckenham
Anna Zair (9)   76
Molly Taylor (9)   77
Jack Newbery (9)   78
Rebecca Holm (9)   79
Kitty Dowry (9)   80
Beth Scrutton (10)   81
Lucy Bounds (9)   82
Emily Buck (9)   83
Liberty Butler (9)   84

Overstone Primary School, Overstone
Roisin Brown (7)   85
Billy Benamore (8)   86
William Pattison (8)   87
Elise Osborne (7)   88
Tayla Halfacre (7)   89
Joshua Hoskin (8)   90
Jared Hoskin (8)   91
Tom Westrep (8)   92
Adam Parkes (8)   93
Ella-Mae Lovesay (8)   94
Ellie-May Steele (7)   95
Aimee Gilkes (9)   96
Charlie Lee (9)   97
Ella Coulton (8)   98
Rachel Taylor (7)   99
Jack Kyprianides (7)   100
Mark John Hardwick (8)   101
Joanna Poole (8)   102
Morgan Holt (7)   103
Jordan May (10)   104
Nicole Thorneycroft (10)   105
Guy Kitchener (10)   106
Martin Nguyen (10)   107
Vicki Peck (9)   108

Georgia Clark (10)	109
Eleanor Russell (10)	110
Harry Lund (10)	111
Laura Griffiths (10)	112
Katie Gurr (9)	113
Harley Holland (9)	114
Lisa Whenman (10)	115
Ellie Houghton (9)	116
Harry Blason (10)	117
Tomas Frohawk (9)	118
Ben Briers (10)	119
Lauren Burgess (9)	120
Charley Benamore (10)	121
Georgia Brown (9)	122
Alexander Pattison (10)	123
Abbie Long (9)	124
Becky Matthews (10)	125

Pixmore Junior School, Letchworth

Kirstie Coe (9)	126
Mary Kitching (10)	127
William Jones (10)	128
Esme Horwood (9)	129
Liam Lock (9)	130
Sarah Anthony (9)	131
Mary Wagnall (9)	132
Matthew Horder (9)	133
Tamar Dulley (9)	134
Annie Summan (9)	135
Adam Fortune (9)	136
Luis Fernandes (7)	137
Elise Ceri Lambert (7)	138
Euan Ryan (7)	139
Kieran Shurmer-Elliott (7)	140
Kia Tarling (8)	141
Scarlett Ross (8)	142
Lauren Carter (7)	143
Danielle Dulley (8)	144
Simon Kitching (7)	145
Jared Guy (7)	146
Claire-Amandine Sempala (7)	147

Joseph Smith (7)   148
Samuel West (7)   149
Sarah Jane Glatzhofer (7)   150
Chad Whitby (7)   151
Ben Dulley (7)   152
Jonathan Batt (7)   153
Jessica Baines (7)   154
Kiera Brunton (7)   155
Leah Summan (8)   156
Adam Carter (8)   157
Ishan Loi (7)   158
Terri Heeks (7)   159
Tanisha-Marie Fountain (7)   160
Kimberley Clarke (7)   161
Asharna Clark (7)   162
Grace Twitchett (7)   163
Lewis White (7)   164
Ruth Fox (7)   165
Aislinn Rainey (7)   166
Akshay Dhunna (7)   167
Gerardo Esposito (7)   168
Joseph Hathway-Neville (7)   169
Kerry Davis (8)   170
Bradley Baynes (8)   171
Rhys Jackson (7)   172
Florence Gorski-Giles (7)   173
Charlie Bohm (7)   174
Darnell Jackson (7)   175
Ruth Bainbridge (9)   176
Sophie Jones (9)   177
Megan Keighley (10)   178
Malachi Lalite (9)   179
Jack Horder (8)   180
Thomas Bunyan (9)   181

St Thomas More Middle School, Norwich
Annabelle Schofield (11)   182
Mollie Armes (11)   183
Rowan Perrow (9)   184
Cleo Anderson (11)   185
Lucy Zhuang (10)   186

The Poems

My Forest

Through the trees small leaves dance
Down to the floor weave, fling and prance
The forest is such a thing to see
A rainbow of colours comes to me
Down the ditches people walk
In the treetops squirrels stalk
When you feel the heat of the sun
It means the old owl's day is done
With the stream long and the trees high
It makes you smile to see a big blue sky
With millions of trees blocking the light
It's calm and peaceful till the night.

Greg Collins (11)

What Would I Be?

I would be a monkey
I would play all day
Sleep late at night
Have a playfight
My mum would groom me
And give me a bath
My dad would watch out
For the naughty giraffes.

Mark Bailey (9)

When I Grow Up

When I grow up
I want to be a dancer
Dancing like a fairy
Pretty hair, nice pink dress
White shoes with bows like my dress
Dancing in the sunlight, moonlight too
Dancing everywhere, even at school.

Courtney Bailey (7)

Playing In The Garden

The sky is blue, it is a sunny day,
In the nice weather we go out to play.
Our garden is a nice big space,
Where we can have a race.
We wear trainers, kick a ball and run,
All of us having a lot of fun.
When we are tired, we go inside and have some tea,
Then we watch television, my mum, dad, sister and me!

Vishakha Lakhani (9)

God

God helps us whatever His name,
He is everywhere, He is the same.
He is inside my body, from head to toe,
God is bright, He can do anything you know!
It is believed that sometimes He takes birth,
To help the people on this Earth.
I hope that He listens to what I say,
Can He stop people killing each other in any way?
Would He teach people to be kind and not kill any living things?
So that one day we may go to Him with His given wings!

Uma Lakhani (9)

Darkness

There was a haunted house!
In the house a bat was hanging from the roof
And a dead man was lying on the stairs.
A door was creaking
And a tap was
Dripping,
Drip,
Drop.

Adam Kilby-Smith (7)
Bedford Preparatory School, Bedford

Hunger

I am hungry,
I need food fast.
I'm bursting for food,
I can't wait any longer.
I'm starving!
I really,
Really,
Need food quickly.
And you know what?
I need a drink as well!

Amir Kalyan (7)
Bedford Preparatory School, Bedford

The Vanishing Sofa

Where is the sofa?
The sofa has gone!
Maybe it went to Mars
Or over the hill and far away.
Where is this silly sofa?
I can't find it anywhere!
Then I get angry,
I am very cross.
I thump and bump,
Then suddenly, I'm not cross.
I stop thumping and bumping.
I see the sofa,
I am happy.
I sit down,
I fall on the floor!
I look around,
The sofa has gone!

Logan Jones (8)
Bedford Preparatory School, Bedford

Darkness

There is something creeping.
Could it be a murderer
Or a werewolf howling?
The cellar is locked!

Darkness,
Darkness.
Zombies coming to get me!
Twigs snapping!
I'm scared!

But at last,
A daredevil,
Saves me!

Harjeet Sumal (8)
Bedford Preparatory School, Bedford

Autumn

Leaves change colour
They fall off the trees
And float down to the ground
When you stamp on them
They crunch and rustle
Days are shorter
Nights are longer
It is damp and misty.

Charles Harrison (7)
Bedford Preparatory School, Bedford

Recipe For Autumn

Take a round, shiny, dark red conker
Add some foggy, wet, muddy leaves
Mix it with some massive pumpkins
And put in five golden, shiny apples
Take stormy, grey smoke from a bonfire
And mist and fog
Harvest corn and make it into bread
Mix it for two days non-stop
Let is set for two days
And it will be the best
The best autumn ever.

Peter Jamieson (8)
Bedford Preparatory School, Bedford

A Recipe For Autumn

Take some solid gold apples
And cut them up into tiny bits
Add the biggest pumpkins in the world
And slice them up into bite size
Mix for six weeks with the stormy fog
And the smoke from a bonfire
And you have made autumn!

Gareth Owens (7)
Bedford Preparatory School, Bedford

Autumn

A mazing, colourful leaves float off the trees
U nusual conkers are found
T umbling to the ground and rolling
U nder the trees
M assive pumpkins are made into pies
N ights are longer and colder.

Oliver McCormack (7)
Bedford Preparatory School, Bedford

Autumn

A nimals start gathering food
U ntidy leaves on the lawn
T idy them up with a rake
U nder the horse chestnut tree are *big* conkers
M any people are having fires
N ot all animals are storing food

I s there room near the fire to warm my hands?
S quirrels are eating nuts

H allowe'en and Bonfire Night
E veryone is out buying fireworks
R abbits are sleeping
E veryone likes autumn.

Edward Zwetsloot (7)
Bedford Preparatory School, Bedford

Recipe For Autumn

Take some golden leaves
On a cold, misty day.
Add some bonfire smoke
Smelling of burning wood.
Mix some shiny conker cases,
That's how to make an autumn day.

Rohan Sanghera (7)
Bedford Preparatory School, Bedford

Autumn

Most leaves change colour in autumn
And float silently to the ground.
When you walk through the leaves,
They munch and crunch and rustle.
It's rainy and damp and dull.
Days get shorter and nights get longer.
Pick some shiny brown conkers
And have a conker fight.

Sachin Patel (7)
Bedford Preparatory School, Bedford

Autumn

Take some big brown conkers
Out of their prickly cases,
Make into delectable pie.
Mix some apples and pears
With some brown and golden leaves,
And you have made autumn.

Freddie Walker (7)
Bedford Preparatory School, Bedford

Autumn

Autumn is here
Leaves fall off the trees
It gets colder and darker
Mist and fog are heading our way
Days are shorter, nights are longer
Put your fire or your heating on
Big, round conkers fall off the trees
Bonfires are lit
Fireworks are let off
Autumn is here.

James Hirst (7)
Bedford Preparatory School, Bedford

Recipe For Autumn

Take some big pumpkins
And some colourful leaves,
Add shiny brown conkers
And black bonfire smoke.
Mix misty fog and red apples,
You have made autumn.

Conrad Staroscik (8)
Bedford Preparatory School, Bedford

Recipe For Autumn

Take a bucket full of leaves
Raked up from the ground
Add some smoke from a campfire
Cooking marshmallows for me to eat
Mix in some apples and pears baked into a pie
And it will always be in autumn.

George Edwards (8)
Bedford Preparatory School, Bedford

A Recipe For Autumn

Take some shiny brown conkers from a horse chestnut tree,
Add some big, tall trees with golden leaves
On a wet, cold, damp day.
Mix with some bonfires and fireworks
And you have made autumn.

James Blane (7)
Bedford Preparatory School, Bedford

A Recipe For Autumn

Take a round, shiny conker
From a horse chestnut tree
Add a few golden leaves
On a damp, rainy day
Mix in some fog
And a bit of black, cloudy smoke
From a bonfire
Add some round orange pumpkins
A few red juicy apples
And a bright yellow pear
And you have made autumn.

Rohan Toor (7)
Bedford Preparatory School, Bedford

Simon's Pets

In his bedroom Simon kept . . .
Five bright green lizards that slither and dash,
Four charging rhinos that barge and crash,
Three graceful horses that gallop and race,
Two chasing cheetahs at full pace,
And one white whale gliding through the water
Like a giant sail.

Simon Beal (8)
Bedford Preparatory School, Bedford

Jonathan's Pets

In his bedroom Jonathan kept . . .
Five angry alligators that hissed and lashed,
Four stripy zebras that zoomed and dashed,
Three ancient sphinxes that roared and growled,
Two death-defying bears that fought and prowled,
And one cuddly cat that always brought me
My one lucky hat!

Jonathan Konstantinidis (8)
Bedford Preparatory School, Bedford

Dexter's Pets

In my bedroom I keep . . .
Five humungous manatees that dance and prance,
Four proactive tigers that growl and prowl,
Three nocturnal bushbabies that nibble and dribble,
Two terrible terrapins that tear and stare
And one irritating brother
And I don't want another!

Dexter Southern (8)
Bedford Preparatory School, Bedford

Darkness

Red eyes when they go *woo, woo,*
An owl when it hoots,
When you hear a monster
It goes *grrrhhh, ooooooo,*
When you're in the dark you hear a *toot, toot*
And you try to go under the duvet
You hear something coming out of the cupboard
You hear somebody coming up the stairs!
I am scared of the darkness.

Stephanos Savvides (7)
Bedford Preparatory School, Bedford

My China Cup

English as the rain that's falling on the ground,
Small as a mouse curled up in a ball,
Hard as a rock that's been cut from a rock,
That's how the world sees me.

I spend my time on a mantel above a flickering fire,
With photos of friends and family,
Watching and waiting to be dusted all clean,
That's how the world sees me.

But in my dreams I belong to the Queen
And every day she fills me up with hot, steaming tea
And I am made of gold, all polished and new.

Spending my time on a great big table
With saucers and spoons all shiny and new,
Knowing that I am a treasure,
That's how I'd like to be.

Honor Gibson
Cadmore End CE Combined School, High Wycombe

Head Up In The Clouds

I am smelly like a bottle of perfume,
That's how the world sees me,

And you will love my heavenly smell
Which I give to your clothes.

I am helpful to get stains out,
That's how the world sees me,

And my idol is Daz,
I hope I grow up to be like him.

But in my dreams I'm washing Madonna's clothes
And I am loved and I spend my time with my best friend.

Charlotte Chapman (10)
Cadmore End CE Combined School, High Wycombe

The Poor Me

Shiny like a piece of gold
Bendy like a piece of Blu-tack
Smooth as a new book
That's how the world sees me.

I spend my time touching a yummy piece of food
With the hot plate boiling away
I am melting and scorching
I am waiting for someone to drop me in a cold cup
That's how the world sees me.

But in my dreams
I am next to my friends -
The spoon, the plate and the knives
Polished and new
Gleaming in the sunlight.

Spending my time in Buckingham Palace
Looking at the Queen
With the fragile forks and the silver spoons
And the golden knives
Knowing that I must be a good object
That's how I'd like to be.

George Horne (10)
Cadmore End CE Combined School, High Wycombe

In My Life

Shiny, like a diamond in the sunlight
Smooth, like a newborn baby's skin
Scratchy as a mad cat
That's how the world sees me.

I spend my time in the dining room
With the table and chairs
Quiet and bored for a couple of minutes
Waiting for someone to use me
That's how the world sees me.

But in my dreams
I am getting used all the time
Polished and new
I will shine evermore.

Spending my time
On the desktop
With people all around me
Knowing the people are caring about me.

Codi Long (10)
Cadmore End CE Combined School, High Wycombe

The Sunshine

Rough, like a hairy wig
Smelly, like an old piece of cheese
Thick, like a churchyard's wall

That's how the world sees me

I spend my time in the kitchen
With my little spoon
Standing and watching for the sun to rise
Waiting for the moon

That's how the world sees me

But in my dreams I'm covered with jewellery
Polished and new
With a crown above to finish me off

Spending my time
Being a princess
With a prince by my side
Knowing that I'd like to hide away
That's how I'd like to be.

Daisy Buckingham (9)
Cadmore End CE Combined School, High Wycombe

In My Dream

Fruity, like a raspberry in the wood
Decorative, like a picture painted by Picasso
Smooth as a hair on a bear's back
That's how the world sees me

I spend my time hoping my lid will be lifted some time soon
With the sugar and salt
Sitting and waiting for my dreams to come true
Waiting for my jar to be filled once again
That's how the world sees me

But in my dreams
I am a pot of Prince Charles
Polished and new
But to him I am special and new

Spending my time sitting on a throne all royal and new
With Camilla and Charles and Prince Harry too
Sitting in the sun, the moon and the stars
Knowing that I will have a happy life.

Megan Poulton
Cadmore End CE Combined School, High Wycombe

In My Dreams

White, like a snowball in the winter
Gold, like a glittery sun moving around the Earth
Shiny as a star falling from the sky
That's how the world sees me.

I would hang on the wall holding bunches of keys
On my hook in the dark cupboard
With a rusty pan next to me
Hanging about and hoping someone will use me.

But in my dreams I would hold the keys to an Aston Martin
Polished and new my hook would be
Spending my time with bunches of keys hanging on me
With my hook as shiny as ever it could be
Knowing that is what I want to be.

Charlie Jones (10)
Cadmore End CE Combined School, High Wycombe

Drink All Up

Bendable, like a rubber
Smooth, like a new page in a book
Bumpy as a bump on a wound-up top
That's how the world sees me

I spend my time in a fridge with food
Hoping someone will use me
Waiting to drink me all up
That's how the world sees me

But in my dreams
On a bike through the woods
Seeing all the lovely trees
Shiny and new as a brand new car

Spending my time
Chilling out in a champagne bucket
That's how the world sees me.

Levi Lee
Cadmore End CE Combined School, High Wycombe

Flower

Bumpy, like a road
Shiny as a diamond in the sun
Soft as a cuddly toy
That's how the world sees me now.

I spend my time on a window sill
With the sun shining on me
Sitting and standing
That's how the world sees me.

But in my dreams I'm an ordinary basket
On the window sill
Polished and new for the Queen to use
Spending my time being filled with flowers
With lots of love
That's how I'd like to be.

Emily Bird (10)
Cadmore End CE Combined School, High Wycombe

Up On The Clouds

Smelly, like a new bottle of soap
Squidgy, like a new baby's hand
Flexible as a piece of string
That's how the world sees me

I spend my time in the utility
With the washing machine crying and sobbing
Waiting for a dip in the sea
That's how the world sees me

But in my dreams I belong to Britney Spears
Washing her baby clothes clean and new
Waiting to be used for people like you
Waiting to have a dip with your dungarees
Knowing that won't happen to me
That's how I'd like to be.

Victoria Penhale (9)
Cadmore End CE Combined School, High Wycombe

Chinese Food

Stripy like a zebra
Blunt like a sword
Smooth as a pebble
That is how the world sees me

I spend my time
In a small, dark drawer
With spoons, knives and crumbs
Hoping someone will order Chinese
That's how the world sees me

But in my dreams I am cut from pine
With a beautiful golden print
Polished and new, used by you
The most special person to me

Spending my time in a gold, silk box
Getting used with great care
Knowing that I am loved again
That's how I'd like to be!

Eleanor Taylor
Cadmore End CE Combined School, High Wycombe

The Sad Me

Wooden, like a cupboard
Hard, like a piano
Round as a ball
That's how the world sees me.

I spend my time in the drawers in the kitchen
With a fork and a knife
Sitting and waiting for someone to use me
Waiting to be helpful
That's how the world sees me.

But in my dreams
I am being used all the time.
Spending my time in the sink
With a plate and a cup
Knowing that I am the only mixer
That's how I'd like to be.

Mikey Sharman-Gutteridge (10)
Cadmore End CE Combined School, High Wycombe

About Me!

Wavy, like a French plait
Woody, like a tree
Portable as a purse
That's how the world sees me.

I spend my time on a shelf
With a flowerpot with roses
Watching Mum doing the washing up
Trying to get off the window ledge
Waiting for picking blueberries
That's how the world sees me.

But in my dreams
I am with my friends in the shop
Polished and new
With Sue and my best friends.

Spending my time
Sometimes on the shop shelf
With teddy bears and toys
Knowing that I will have a home
That's how I'd like to be.

April Coyle (10)
Cadmore End CE Combined School, High Wycombe

Use Me, Don't Lose Me

Cold, like a lonely iceberg
Shiny, like a clean window
Strange as a young baby's language
That's how the world sees me.

I spend my time in the cutlery drawer
With my cutlery friends
Sitting and waiting to be used
Waiting for my body to be warm
That's how the world sees me.

But in my dreams
I am used every day
To cook the Queen's breakfast
Polished and new every time I am used.
Spending my time warm as ever,
Sat by the cooker, shiny and new
With my new friends, the cook and the frying pan
Knowing that I am the cook's favourite tool
That's how I'd like to be.

Brogan Carpenter (11)
Cadmore End CE Combined School, High Wycombe

Want To

Metal, like a car
Bent, like a tent
Round as a cloud
That's how the world sees me

I spend my time
Hung up with a tea towel
Sitting and waiting for someone
For someone to pick me up
Waiting to get taken from this place
That's how the world sees me

But in my dreams
I am in a car or in a lock
Polished and new, as clean as a shoe

Spending my time
In a rusty, old cupboard
With a tea towel
Knowing that will be used
One day that's how I'd like to be.

Joshua Croxford
Cadmore End CE Combined School, High Wycombe

Happy Now, But Not Happy Now

Smooth, like a flower in the breeze
Rough, like a toothbrush
Noisy as a whistle
That's how the world sees me

I spend my time in a key box
Roaring away with my old key
Listening and dreaming
Waiting for people to pick me up and use me
That's how the world sees me

But in my dreams
I am with a pop star in their car
Polished and new
Going to an awards show

Spending my time in a pop star's car
With my key box sitting there in someone's pocket
Knowing that's what I want to do
That's how I'd like to be.

Annabelle Penhale (9)
Cadmore End CE Combined School, High Wycombe

The Food Bin

Colourful, like a rainbow
Smooth, like a baby's bottom
Decorative as a play toy

I spend my time in a box
With Zara's old baby clothes
Waiting to be used
Sitting and waiting
For someone to come and get me
Waiting for the sound of footsteps
That's how I'd like to be

But in my dreams
I am in the Queen's playpen
With her child
Polished and new
It is so good to be back in the open

Spending my time with food on me
And lots of yummy things
With peas, carrots, potatoes, beef
And yummy gravy and that is all
Knowing that the baby loves me
That's how I'd like to be.

Zara Hale (10)
Cadmore End CE Combined School, High Wycombe

Money, Money!

There once was a man called James Funny,
He wished he had lots of money.
People called him Mr Buts,
Because he did not have guts.

He said to them,
He would break the gem,
He was very mysterious,
We knew he was not serious.

I hope you liked the story about him,
Oh yeah, he was very slim.
He went to a bar to find a jar with money,
But all he could find was honey.

He was sly like a fox,
But one day he got the chickenpox.
I hope you liked the story,
The next one will be gory.

Saskia Caddock (9)
Clare Middle School, Clare

Dying For Pie

There once was someone called Thomas Johnsence,
Who was a complete and utter nonsense.
He had but one dream, did you know?
To have his dream, he'd run to and fro.

The dream he had, the big fat lad,
He would die for one big slice of blueberry pie!
Apple pie, raspberry pie,
The amount he ate would make you cry.

He was so big, what a pig,
The way he ate it, it would make you feel sick.
He is so big, you'd think he'd explode,
Probably make the world *kaplode*.

Enough about him,
Let's not talk about this greedy sin.
Pardon, you want to hear the story?
OK, but it's very gory.

Once he went to a shop,
But something caught his eye and made him stop.
It was cream that made you thin
And it was pie flavour, so he went in.
(He wasn't a very good saver.)

That night he put on the cream and screamed,
'I smell so nice, I could eat myself. *Help!*'
In the morning, there was no yawning.

I felt like crying, I tried to tell you,
I was trying and trying.
So that is the end, a horrid bend,
I'm sorry if it was too gory, now that's the end of the story.

Amelia Dzioba (9)
Clare Middle School, Clare

Roses

R oses are special with a wonderful smell,
O h, I love all roses so, so much.
S ometimes I wonder what they're thinking,
E very day I come and look to see if they're OK.
S ometimes I tell my rose how much I love it.
   I love my rose and my rose loves me!

Emily Goodwin (9)
Clare Middle School, Clare

Weird And Wonderful!

Fairies, pixies, elves and wizards,
Witches, owls and a great big blizzard.
Anyone, even you, could see them if you wanted to.
Lions, tigers, bears 'n' all,
Could go with you to a Chinese ball.
You see the leopard, yellow and spotty,
It's just a shame the birds aren't dotty.
Funny that, isn't it?
Ha, ha, ha, what a twit.
I do like this poem, do you agree?
Oh, do you like climbing big green trees?
Cos I do, yippee!
By the way, bye-bye from me,
Bye from me.

Cydney Nunn (9)
Clare Middle School, Clare

School

S chool is fun
C lasses are sometimes boring
H aving funny times with teachers
O ld school smells all funny
O ur swimming pool is green (yuck!)
L oving all the school, lots and lots.

Charlotte Bareham (9)
Clare Middle School, Clare

Art, Art - Cinquain

Art, art,
Really messy.
A fantastic project,
But you can never get it wrong.
Art, art.

Rhianna Dourado (9)
Clare Middle School, Clare

The Medical Genius

The medical genius had a breakthrough,
He went to try it out at the zoo.
He won a game of chess,
Got a ride on the pony express.
It was anybody's guess
Where he was after Loch Ness.
He got married to a princess,
He went on a quest,
To find a fancy dress test
And we don't know the rest.

Eleanor Rodwell-Cullup (10)
Clare Middle School, Clare

My Planets

As the moons of Jupiter,
Twirl round and round,
An alien flies in a spaceship,
Not making a sound.

Saturn's rings get
Bigger each day,
In a galaxy called
The Milky Way.

Earth's inhabitants are
Having a war,
Somewhere in Ecuador
With a dinosaur!

Mercury is a small planet,
But very, very hot,
Only one man has been there
And his name is Lancelot.

Uranus' rings are small but long
And you cannot see them,
In the middle of the planet hidden away,
There is a secret gem.

James Curran   (9)
Clare Middle School, Clare

The Voyage Of The Polka Dot Prawn

There was a prawn in a sailor's hat,
Who went to sea with a couple of cats.

When he went home to see his mum,
She turned round and smacked his bum.

When he went back out to sea,
The cat said, 'I need a pee.'

The prawn had never heard such a thing,
When he looked at his boat, it had wings.

Then the prawn had polka dot spots,
At least he will until he rots.

Max Murphy (10)
Clare Middle School, Clare

Rhymes

R hymes are like a short story
H appiness is not like gory
Y oung like to read easy books
M aybe for adults who like to look
E very book has at least one picture
S o every poet is a little bit richer.

Emily-Ann Caton (9)
Clare Middle School, Clare

Rhyming

R hyming is great
H ave you done some rhyming lately?
Y ou should rhyme a lot like me
M y pen has nearly run out because I rhyme so much
I rhyme a lot
N o, you don't need rhyming in a poem
G o and do some rhyming now.

Sam Ager (9)
Clare Middle School, Clare

Trev, The One-Legged Troll

The one-legged troll is an ordinary man,
In the coldest of winters he eats strawberry flan.
He has just one leg where he wears a boot
And he has a piano, guitar and flute.
Seeing people eat flan makes him go green,
But it gets even worse when they're eating baked beans.

From him you must run as fast as you can,
For he likes eating strawberry flan!

Adam Chinery (10)
Clare Middle School, Clare

Enchanted Wood

In the enchanted wood
Fairies fly, dragons live
And monsters run and dance
Ride a dragon if you could
In the enchanted wood.

Purple trees and mountains high
Dirty trolls gliding by
Berries talk
And red eagles fly
In the enchanted wood.

When you're angry, the trees turn red
When you're sad, they turn blue
But when you're happy, they are golden brown
So if you could,
Visit the magical, splendorous, happy, enchanted wood

Where toadstools sing
And palm trees hum
Where flowers la-la-la
You will have an enchanting time in the enchanted wood.

Autumn Wulff (10)
Clare Middle School, Clare

Christmas!

C is for crackers that crack when they're opened
H is for holly that makes people jolly
R is for reindeer that run through the snow
I is for icicles that drip from the roof
S is for Santa who comes in the night
T is for tinsel that hangs on the tree
M is for mistletoe you kiss underneath
A is for amazing lights that spell out messages
S is for snow that covers the churches.

Claire Morey (10)
Clare Middle School, Clare

Seasons

Seasons come and seasons go,
Winter is the snow.

Summer is the warm sun,
There for everyone.

Springtime is the Mayday Fair,
Baby animals in their mothers' care.

Autumn is the crinkly leaves,
Falling down from the trees.

All the seasons play their part,
They all have a special place in my heart.

Harriet Potter (9)
Clare Middle School, Clare

Mum

I like my mum,
She is very nice.
She's not fun,
But still, she's a lovely mum.

Billy Guiry (9)
Clare Middle School, Clare

Spaniel

S uper dogs
P roper English dogs
A nd they drive you crazy
N aughty
I nto playing
E ndless sprinting
L oving and kind.

Ben Rawlings (9)
Clare Middle School, Clare

Why Come To Our Beach?

Beaches are quiet or noisy!
Every wave is a different height
And every piece of sand is different.
Come, come, come to our beach!
Here we have huts to rent or buy.
Even babies and couples come to our beach.
So come to our beach for your holiday!

All our ice cream is lovely.
Really, we are the best.
Every time you pay a certain amount, get discount!

Fun doesn't cover our beach.
Unique style is what we have.
Never go to another beach
Because we are the *best!*

Elspeth Walker (9)
Clare Middle School, Clare

A Pocketful Of Rhyme

D aisies are precious flowers, full of magic inside their roots
A s long as they can stay so pretty for a flower, I am happy
I am so happy with the daisies and me
S ometimes I wonder how daisies flower because they are pretty
Y ou should love daisy flowers too, cos I sure do!

Paige Mylchreest (9)
Clare Middle School, Clare

Saddle - Cinquain

Saddle,
Sometimes rusty,
Mine is never rusty,
But Victoria's always is!
Horses.

Ellen Beattie (9)
Clare Middle School, Clare

Food

A pples are healthy
B ananas are yellow
C risps are crunchy
D oughnuts are doughy
E ggs are small
F ish is fishy
G ingerbread men are tasty
H ot dogs are hot
I ce cream is cold
J am is jammy
K iwi is sweet
L emon is sour
M elon is chewy
N uts are nutty
O ranges are sticky
P izza is lovely
Q uavers are cheesy
R ice is nice
S ausages are chewy
T omatoes are messy
U gli fruit is ugly
V imto is fizzy
W ater is cool
X o sauce is nice
Y oghurt is delightful
Z ap ice lollies are cold.

Marcus Brooker (10)
Clare Middle School, Clare

The Sunset Cycle - Haiku

The water lies still
As the sunset is creeping
The night comes awake.

Madeleine Warnes (9)
Great Casterton CE Primary School, Great Casterton

Smudge - Haiku

Smudge is very cute
She loves her scrumptious treats too
I love her to bits.

Aimee West (9)
Great Casterton CE Primary School, Great Casterton

Slowly The Night

Slowly the night creeps within the farm,
As if a dragon, riding madly,
Swoops down with claws like fingers
And wings like pixie ears,
Listening for its prey in the deep darkness,
Its evil shining down on the small, dusty road.

Melissa Eddisford (9)
Great Casterton CE Primary School, Great Casterton

Slowly The Night

Slowly the night creeps within the fierce dragon,
Widen to the moonlight, breathing darkness like fire,
Past the glimmering, orange sunset
And the dark, unseen fields,
Down the long village,
Slowly the night, creeping, creeping,
Claws clutching, wings wide,
A dragon looking for the fire.

Charlie Parker & Jodie Hunt (9)
Great Casterton CE Primary School, Great Casterton

Slowly The Giant

Giant creeping over the hills
Dragging the midnight sky with him
Covering the world with his black cloak.

Jack Woodhouse & Thomas Watterson (9)
Great Casterton CE Primary School, Great Casterton

Apples

Bunches of juicy apples on the mushroom-shaped tree,
All to share for you and me.
All the apples that you like,
Are all in sight for you to bite.

Hollie Raeburn (11)
Great Casterton CE Primary School, Great Casterton

Rabbit

Rabbits
Rabbit sleek and soft
Peeking through the loft

Rabbits big, rabbits small
Rabbits in the dark hall

Rabbits here, rabbits there
Rabbits almost everywhere

Some rabbits are silky
Some rabbits are small
Some rabbits are not afraid at all.

Ellen Roke (9)
Great Casterton CE Primary School, Great Casterton

Space

Space is black
With stars that shine.
Rockets zoom past
Very fast.
Lots of planets
Different colours
From red to green,
Spacemen floating so serene.
The sun, the moon,
Circle the Earth,
Could this be your doom?
Pluto blue, Mars red,
Cosmic dust around my head.

Jessica Harrison (9)
Great Casterton CE Primary School, Great Casterton

Haikus

Ponies:
Ponies on the hill
Grazing on the luscious grass
In the summer's heat.

Autumn days:
In the autumn days
Leaves falling from trees on high
Golden, brown and green.

The seaside breeze:
The big seaside breeze
Weaves through the big crowds at night
And grasps the night stars.

Laura Hartshorne (10)
Great Casterton CE Primary School, Great Casterton

Our Teacher

Coffee drinker,
Website linker.

Messy writer,
Classroom lighter.

Trip taker,
Plate breaker.

Homework giver,
Science siever

Tea spiller,
Big grinner.

Book reader,
Plant seeder.

Nature lover,
Good mother.

She is a type of creature,
But she is our teacher.
Mrs Cleaves.

Francesca Cooper (9)
Great Casterton CE Primary School, Great Casterton

You Can Rap

You can rap to the king
You can rap to the queen
You can rap to the children
You can rap in-between.

Larna Thorpe (9)
Great Casterton CE Primary School, Great Casterton

Seasons

In spring
You feel like you're going to ping
Ping up, ping down
With flowers all around
To butterflies flying
To trained men sky-diving
That's why we all like spring.

In summer
It is hot
And you eat ice creams a lot
When you laugh the day away
You say, 'Have I wasted that? Oh bother!'

In autumn
When the rain falls
The conkers will fall
And the children will collect them
The wind will blow
And the stream will flow.

In winter
The white, bright sun
Glistens on the frost
Outside there's a wizard blizzard
All is silent
The only noise is the thud of snow.

Anna Zair (9)
Old Buckenham Community Primary School, Old Buckenham

What Am I?

I suck things up
And empty things out
I make things clean
But you can take me about
I have a long, thin body
With a thin, sucking mouth
I have teeth that are black
And go forward and back
The noise that I make
Is loud and clear
But I most definitely can't
Suck up pints of beer.

Molly Taylor (9)
Old Buckenham Community Primary School, Old Buckenham

Poem Time

My brother knows a boy called Dan
And his dad has a very big van.
He said, 'Goodness me!'
When he drove into a tree.
Now Dan is an injured man.

Jack Newbery (9)
Old Buckenham Community Primary School, Old Buckenham

Stars

Shining brightly,
Twirling around,
Above in the sky
And not on the ground.

Rebecca Holm (9)
Old Buckenham Community Primary School, Old Buckenham

People

People are lovely and sweet,
They joke around at parties,
Some people are happy and sad,
Some people are cross.

Kitty Dowry (9)
Old Buckenham Community Primary School, Old Buckenham

What Am I?

I'm silky and shiny
And not very tiny,
I eat little fish,
That's my favourite dish,
I swim with my friends,
The fun never ends.
What am I?
A dolphin.

Beth Scrutton (10)
Old Buckenham Community Primary School, Old Buckenham

My Animals

My pony's called Midnight
She sparkles in the moonlight
And I have a dog called Jessie
Who is always very messy
And I have a dog called Tilly
And she is really silly
I have a dog called Polly
She is a bit of a wally.

Lucy Bounds (9)
Old Buckenham Community Primary School, Old Buckenham

The Seasons

It is spring and I see the trees blossoming
I smell the flowers bursting out
I feel the grass beneath my toes.

It is summer and I see blazing sunshine on me
I hear trees whistling softly
I smell the lovely cut grass
I feel the breeze whistling calmly.

It is autumn and I see the different coloured leaves
I hear the leaves floating down
I smell the cold air
I feel the crispy leaves crackling in my fingers.

It is winter and I see the white crystal sheets covering the land
I hear the ice cracking under my feet
I smell the misty, cold air
I feel the cold snow under my toes.

Emily Buck (9)
Old Buckenham Community Primary School, Old Buckenham

Who Are We?

We have different jobs,
But we all chew food.
Even though it's a job,
We can never get sued.
Unless you don't clean us
With a toothbrush and paste,
You'll get a filling,
Which you'll have to face!

Liberty Butler (9)
Old Buckenham Community Primary School, Old Buckenham

What Is The Sun?

The sun is a Catherine Wheel
Spinning in the light morning sky
Ripening the corn
As the day goes by.

It is a bright red tomato
Rolling in the warm afternoon sky
Toasting our backs
As we ride on by.

It's a pink, bouncy hopper
Drifting away
Through the darkening sky
Slowly fading, waving us goodbye.

Roisin Brown (7)
Overstone Primary School, Overstone

Untitled

10, 9, 8, 7, 6, 5, 4, 3, 2, 1, lift-off
They start the race
The two rockets shoot into space
They go past Mars
See the stars
Go down to the launch pad
That was great.

Billy Benamore (8)
Overstone Primary School, Overstone

My Favourite Pastimes

I love to play tennis
With a little boy called Dennis
We are part of a squad
And it doesn't feel very odd.

I am in the mini greens
'Cause I am so very keen
They call me a little star
And say I will go far.

Dad has made me play rugby
So that people will not mug me
I started to learn karate
But would rather be at a party.

I really would like to be a basketball player
But Mum says I haven't a prayer
We have to get there at 8 sharp
But I am still eating my Pop Tarts.

My very best pastime of all
Is sitting in front of the TV driving my dad up the wall
He has high hopes for me
But all I want to be is Mike TV.

William Pattison (8)
Overstone Primary School, Overstone

About My Dog

I have a dog, his name is Jack,
His coat is soft and white and black.

He likes to play,
He likes to play all day.

Jack likes to chew on bones and shoes
And chairs and ice cream cones.

He barks at everyone in the street,
'Stop it, Jack! Here's a treat!'

He barks at the rabbit in her hutch,
But I still love my puppy very, very much!

Elise Osborne (7)
Overstone Primary School, Overstone

The Holiday!

I went to Spain
On a big plane,
The weather was great
I stayed up late.

The sea was blue
I built sandcastles too,
I swam in the pool
Because it made me cool.

It was a great holiday
With my dad and mum,
But I'm glad to be back
Because I missed my sums.

Tayla Halfacre (7)
Overstone Primary School, Overstone

Untitled

I looked up in the air
And saw a snake gliding there
Up and down it went
Its body twisted and bent
Flying quick as a jet
I bet.

Joshua Hoskin (8)
Overstone Primary School, Overstone

Untitled

Slithery, slimy snake
Looking for a bite
Slithering up your back
Giving you such a fright.

Jared Hoskin (8)
Overstone Primary School, Overstone

I Am 8 Today

Birthday cake is my favourite
I love the icing
Ripping open presents
Tripping over the paper
Having lots to eat
Dancing with my friends
Anyone want more cake?
Yes!

Tom Westrep (8)
Overstone Primary School, Overstone

Star Freckles

1, 2, 3, 4, 5, lift-off
Rocket roaring, rocket soaring
Flying high into the sky
That's so pretty
Do you see those stars?
The moon, the stars and Mars
The stars are twinkling
Making freckles in the sky.

Adam Parkes (8)
Overstone Primary School, Overstone

Dancing

I love dancing lots and lots
Buns and clips in my hair
Tap, tap, tapping my shoes
When it stops, that's not fair!

Ballet, tap, modern and jazz
Pinks and purples, pirouettes and whirls
Pliés, kicks, gallops and jumps
Pretty and frilly tutus on dainty girls.

Ella-Mae Lovesay (8)
Overstone Primary School, Overstone

Butterflies Or Flutterbys?

B utterfly, butterflies everywhere
U nusual wings, always in a pair
T rying not to fly into the spider's lair
T urning and twisting out of a cocoon
E xpect to see them around the month of June
R ed Admirals, peacock, small and large white
F lutterbys, butterflies? What a beautiful sight
L ovely and graceful, gliding in the sky
Y es, I love to see a butterfly flutter by.

Ellie-May Steele (7)
Overstone Primary School, Overstone

Rainbows

I love to look at rainbows in the sky,
As they burst through the clouds with their rays of light.
Oh why do you have to be so way up high?
You are so magical, wonderful and bright.

You make rainy days special by shining through,
You make me smile and that's why I love you.
All of your colours are so beautiful and bold,
I wish I could find your pot of gold!

Aimee Gilkes (9)
Overstone Primary School, Overstone

My New Bedroom

In my bedroom one wall is red,
I also have a silver bunk bed.
I have a big TV and an Xbox,
And a chest of drawers for my boxers and socks.
On my wall is a picture of Daisy,
She's our dog, who is very lazy.

Charlie Lee (9)
Overstone Primary School, Overstone

If I Was A Star In The Sky

If I was a star in the sky
I would shine so bright
To light up all the gardens
In the middle of the night.
The animals would be able
To watch their children play
So that they would be ready
To sleep in the day.
My light would shine
On everyone
And I would grant every wish
To make them happy.

Ella-Louise Coulton (8)
Overstone Primary School, Overstone

Blossom

Blossom is a flower
It is also my guinea pig
I love my guinea pig
She is so cute and sweet
And most importantly
She is the best.

Rachel Taylor (7)
Overstone Primary School, Overstone

Monkeys

Monkeys are cute
Monkeys are sweet
Bananas are things
They really like to eat.
They swing through the trees
And pick each other's fleas
Yes, monkeys are cute
I'm sure you'll agree.

Jack Kyprianides (7)
Overstone Primary School, Overstone

Zippy

Zippy is so cute, you have to hug her,
When you hug her, you hear her purr.
She squawks when she wants to go outside,
When she's outside she hides.
She runs like a leopard
And she might pounce on something green,
And she might not be seen.

Mark John Hardwick (8)
Overstone Primary School, Overstone

All About My Year

My name is Joanna
And I'm in Year 4.
If you ask me,
I'll knock on your door.
I am eight,
I am never late.
I like to cook
And read a book.
I take my part
And I do art.
Numeracy and literacy,
It must be.
Year 4,
It's for me.

Joanna Poole (8)
Overstone Primary School, Overstone

My Dog Called Sammy

We take her over the park
My dog called Sammy
When she sees a squirrel
She always has to bark.

Morgan Holt (7)
Overstone Primary School, Overstone

What Have We Done To Our World?

What have we done to our world?
All the rubbish we've hurled
The carbon monoxide and carbon dioxide
What have we done to our world?

All the fumes from your car
The end can't be far
The acid rain, the fumes of a flame
What have we done to our world?

The ozone layer's breaking
Because the aerosols are spraying
The smoke of the power stations is wiping out our nations
What have we done to our world?

The days are hot like a kiln
So hot that it can kill
The polar ice caps are melting, for animals this is not helping
What have we done to our world?

The sea levels are rising
Because the ice caps are melting
Soon we'll all be drowned because there is no ground
What have we done to our world?

Jordan May (10)
Overstone Primary School, Overstone

Spring Poem

Spring is where the flower grows
This is where the river flows
Which makes the grass grow
The trees bend into a pretty bow

In spring the sky is sometimes grey
Which makes it rain nearly every day
Spring is in May
And everyone likes to say hooray!

Nicole Thorneycroft (10)
Overstone Primary School, Overstone

My Family

I have the funniest family, honest and true,
Here I'll introduce them to you.

My mum is mad and so is my dad,
They sing and dance, oh what a perform-ance.

My dog is called Jack, he is white and black,
(Not really, he's brown.)
He does nothing all day but bark and play,
He just loves to sleep and onto my bed he will sneak.

My dad is so tall, handsome and bold
And he plays cricket for the village of Old.

My mum thinks she's gorgeous, witty and kind,
But I know she's just out of her mind!

Well, I am the son of this family,
Everyone's mad, except for *me!*

Guy Kitchener (10)
Overstone Primary School, Overstone

My Favourite Places

My favourite place is my bedroom,
Where I grow my wings and set free,
It's very nice and relaxing
And very special to me.

My favourite place is my lounge,
It adds pleasure and happiness to my life,
Where I'm calm, grateful and full of excitement,
I love my lounge, it's very nice.

My favourite place is my garden,
I play lots of games like sport,
It keeps me energetic,
But it's not as big as some sort.

My favourite place is my school,
I meet and greet a friend,
It gives me education,
I won't be happy when it comes to an end.

Even though my life isn't perfect,
I sometimes make mistakes,
But even so I will love it forever
And never give up, whatever it takes.

Martin Nguyen (10)
Overstone Primary School, Overstone

The First Day Back To School

'It is the first day back to school!' I cried,
Opening my eyes wide.

Then I began to feel sick,
When Mum said, 'Get up, Vic.'

I was still feeling sick when I got in the car,
I got there so quick even though it was so far.

I was trying to be brave,
But I felt like I was trapped in a cave.

When I saw my friends I began to feel less afraid,
And soon we were laughing together as we played.

Then the bell rang and it was time to go in,
I got a scared and excited feeling.

I walked to the classroom and sat down,
Nervously I looked around.

After the register we lined up by the wall,
Then walked into assembly in the school hall.

This year I am able to sit on a bench
Rather than the grubby old floor,
I felt very grown up and I can see a lot more.

The receptions started for the morning,
They looked so cute and adoring.

I felt like a teenager compared to them,
Sadly, they went home at 12pm.

It now feels like I've never been away
And I never had a six-week holiday.

Vicki Peck (9)
Overstone Primary School, Overstone

In The Light Of The Morning

In the light of the morning,
As I rub my eyes, yawning,
I feel hopeful and bright,
Everything seems right.

By the cold dark of night,
I know nothing is right,
When children are starving
And everyone is at war.

As I fall asleep in my bed,
It all runs through my head,
But I know how to cope,
Because tomorrow brings hope.

Georgia Clark (10)
Overstone Primary School, Overstone

The Weather

It has been raining all day long,
So I sing my favourite song.
As the sun reappears,
All the rain just disappears.
I like the sun to shine all day,
All my troubles just float away.

When it rains it's dull and boring,
I am so bored, I start snoring.
When it's sunny, it's bright and clear,
The birds are chirping which you can hear.
Everyone's happy when it's sunny,
But when it's raining, they seem funny.

When it rains it wriggles down your back,
It even seeps through any crack.
When it rains you get soaking wet
And in fact so does your pet.
Last of all I have to say,
When it rains it ruins your day!

Eleanor Russell (10)
Overstone Primary School, Overstone

The Dog Called Sam

There was once a dog called Sam,
He liked to eat a lot of ham.
He would sleep all day
And sleep all night,
Then in the morning
He would go for a bite.

Harry Lund (10)
Overstone Primary School, Overstone

Poppy

I've got a cat called Poppy
She is also my friend
When she's around people, she's very soppy
And we always play pretend.

She's getting very old
But she's my good old gal
I make sure that she is told
That she's my very best pal.

Laura Griffiths (10)
Overstone Primary School, Overstone

My Friends

My friends are the best, I think they're very cool,
They don't very often stress, we hang out at the swimming pool.
Me and my best friend, Abbie, we always play with the boys,
They always catch us and nick all our toys.
Some of my friends are very tall and some of them are very small,
We sometimes fall out a bit, but then we make up.
They sometimes sit on the friendship bench,
But then I go up and help them.
I am a very good friend to them, I would never let them down,
Whenever they're sad, I act like a clown,
Then they would never feel down.

Katie Gurr (9)
Overstone Primary School, Overstone

Being Me!

Big bugs, ugly bugs,
I love them all.
Creepy things, stingy things,
Anything that crawls.
Messy hair, dirty knees,
Climbing up a tree.
Dirty face, happy face,
Definitely me!
Moonies in the garden,
Making my friends giggle.
Leaving messes everywhere,
Getting in a pickle.
Having fun, running about,
Screaming, laughing, jump and shout.
Rugby tackles and being free,
It is just *great* being me!

Harley Holland (9)
Overstone Primary School, Overstone

The Reader Of This Poem

(Inspired by 'The Writer of this Poem' by Roger McGough)

The reader of this poem,
Is as quick as lightning,
As tall as a tree
And is exceptionally frightening!

As daft as a brush,
Chewy as gum,
Laughs like a hyena,
As bossy as my mum!

As salty as the sea,
Soft as a feather,
Looks like a rhino
And smells like leather!

They're as bright as a bulb,
Lighter than air,
Is a master criminal,
So better beware!

Lisa Whenman (10)
Overstone Primary School, Overstone

Autumn Is Here

Autumn is here, the leaves are falling,
Autumn is here, leaves are coloured yellow, brown,
Orange, gold and red.
Autumn is here, collect all the leaves in a big pile
That touches the sky.
Autumn is here, the leaves crackle like crisps
Crumbling in your mouth.
Autumn is here, the conkers are falling,
Let's see how many we can find.
Autumn is here, hit the conkers with a stick
And make a pile.
Autumn is fading, trees are sleeping,
Conkers are moulding.
Say goodbye to autumn because it's going now,
Bye-bye.

Ellie Houghton (9)
Overstone Primary School, Overstone

Winter

Sparkling snow floating to the ground,
Bare trees swaying in the breeze,
Jack Frost creeps without a sound,
Stripping the leaves from the trees,
Sitting by the fire warming up,
Darkness drawing in,
Drinking cocoa from a cup,
Animals so quietly hibernate,
As food is hard to find,
Birds fly far to migrate
And leave the howling blizzards behind.

Harry Blason (10)
Overstone Primary School, Overstone

Tom's Bomb

There was a boy named Tom
Who made a flour bomb
He threw it into the air
And it landed in his hair

His mum yelled, 'Off to bed!'
And his dad said, 'Without any bread.'
Granny wailed, 'That child's a disgrace.'
Grandad was laughing all over his face

In the morning his hair was stiff
So his grandad made it into a quiff
Off to school Tom did roam
But Mr Currell sent him home.

Tomas Frohawk (9)
Overstone Primary School, Overstone

My Hero, Doctor Who

The ever-changing Time Lord travels
Through time and space
Barcelona, London, Utah, Klom or
Galafray, who knows
When or where?

Metal monsters making mincemeat
Of human-like life forms
With cries of 'exterminate' or 'delete'!

Rose, Mikey, K9 and others
All join up with the mystery man
With two hearts and no home
To save the planet Earth
That they live on today.

Ben Briers (10)
Overstone Primary School, Overstone

Autumn Night

As the leaves fall off the trees,
The night begins to darken.
It's getting cold,
So I was told to make sure
That I go to sleep
Before the last dog has barken.
I don't like the breeze,
Then I start to sneeze
And I have to wipe my nose.
Oh dear, I think I have a cold.
I think it might rain,
I will have to get my umbrella out
Before I go out again.

Lauren Burgess (9)
Overstone Primary School, Overstone

Winter's Day

Winter's day when snow starts to fall,
People no longer going in their swimming pools,
Snowmen seen everywhere,
Winter hats covering hair,
Children playing in the snow,
Water in rivers will no longer flow,
Bare trees all around,
Ice all over on the ground,
All animals are asleep,
Dead leaves in little heaps,
Spring comes out from his winter sleep,
Winter gives a little weep.

Charley Benamore (10)
Overstone Primary School, Overstone

My Roses

Roses are red
Violets are blue
I love flowers
They're so cool
I see them growing
All around the school.

Georgia Brown (9)
Overstone Primary School, Overstone

My Holidays

For my summer holiday we went to Spain,
We got there in an aeroplane.
It took no time at all,
Now we can start having a ball!

We hired a car with seven seats,
So our family could fit nice and neat.
We went for a swim and learnt how to dive,
I am so glad that I am still alive!

We went to the seaside and played in the sand
And listened to the faraway band.
My brother and I dug a hole,
As big as can be, just like a mole.

I had a large Pepsi, then needed a wee,
So I thought I might have a swim in the sea.
But the fish swam towards me,
So I ran out as quick as can be.

We made lots of friends at the sea
And I hope they will keep in touch with me.
But now it's time to end my little rhyme
To get to our plane on time.

Alexander Pattison (10)
Overstone Primary School, Overstone

My Cat Whiskers

Whiskers is my kitten
She is very sweet
She follows me around the house
Purring at my feet.
Chicken is her favourite treat
She has it every week
She likes to sleep a lot
And rest her tired feet.
When she wakes her sleepy eyes
She runs around making lots of mess
But we don't care
She's the best.

Abbie Long (9)
Overstone Primary School, Overstone

Children

Children just love it when they go out to play,
But when they have work they moan away.
They love their fizzy drinks and their food,
But when it is time for bed, they get into a mood.

They love their sisters and also their brothers,
They love their fathers and their mothers.
They hate the smoochy kisses and tight hugs,
They try to run away, but it is no use, they're loved!

Becky Matthews (10)
Overstone Primary School, Overstone

The Lonely Puppy

A cold, lonely night
A puppy full of fright
A rubbish-strewn street
Dirty body and aching feet

A city huge and very scary
The poor animal not very daring
Abandoned puppy, small and thin
Raising up his bristly chin

Left outside all alone
Making his innocent squeaky tone
A damp, scared, dirty puppy
Squeaking, hoping just to be lucky.

Kirstie Coe (9)
Pixmore Junior School, Letchworth

The Blitz

Bombs crashing
Rattles sounding
People running
Wardens shouting

Crying in the air raid shelters
Buzzing overhead
German planes flying over
Going away to leave the dead

Houses crumbled
Fires raged
People left homes
In the blaze . . .

Blitz!

Mary Kitching (10)
Pixmore Junior School, Letchworth

Feeling Ill

Bang! goes my headache,
Swallow! goes my throat,
Echo! goes my voice box,
Smash! as my eyes close,
Peace! as my head hits my pillow.

William Jones (10)
Pixmore Junior School, Letchworth

The Forest

Big black bears, heavy and huge,
Three little baby bears pretending they're dudes,
Groups of bears pace through the forest,
The trees are getting cut down, being demolished.
Furry bodies dip under the waterfall,
Black babies curl up in a ball,
Rabbits hop about on the lush green grass,
Galloping antelopes rush past.
Big huge bears snarl, protecting their babies,
Wild dogs run around with rabies,
Birds fly from the trees,
Howling wolves fall on their knees.

Esme Horwood (9)
Pixmore Junior School, Letchworth

My Chinchillas

My chinchillas are very cute
My chinchillas are very plumpy
In the day they are mute
But at night they are jumpy.

Besides being cute they are fragile
Some are small
They are all agile
And let's just say they jump storeys tall.

Just like Olympians they are really strong
I love them all as a friend
To hate them would be really wrong
And that's my poem, it's the end.

Liam Lock (9)
Pixmore Junior School, Letchworth

The Panda

The endangered species strolls on the Chinese land
Whilst its only friend rolls on the golden sand
It munches on a lush green tree
And feels so happy to be free

The panda cushions its fur patched white
And its playful best friend goes out of sight
The tropical breeze goes through its hair
Then its friend jumps out and gives it a dare

They ran together over to the shade
And rolled around, then comfortably laid
They watched the clouds go by and by
They then gave out a panda sigh!

Sarah Anthony (9)
Pixmore Junior School, Letchworth

The Beautiful Butterfly

Look, what's passing by?
A great big innocent butterfly,
Flapping in the trees,
Blowing in the blustery breeze.

I've watched you for an hour,
Posed against a purple flower,
It's like you're fast asleep,
Or silently starting to weep.

Your wings are starting to droop,
But then you loop-the-loop,
Flying across the ebony-black sea,
Then you find a golden key.

I'll remember you forever,
Lying in a bed of heather,
I want to keep you as a pet,
Like I have since we've met.

Mary Wagnall (9)
Pixmore Junior School, Letchworth

Diseases, Pollution, Poverty!

There once was a shining knight far from the Africas,
Who wanted to wipe out these terrible terrors,
Of pollution, diseases and preposterous poverty,
The townsfolk thought it was a funny novelty.

He fought his way through mystical creatures,
Then sought some advice from a magical tree preacher,
This magical tree felt sorry for this man,
Who really had a lot on his hands.

This magical tree sent him on his way saying,
'Be careful when you get to immortal quay,
There are zombies there unloading boats
And in the boxes are poisonous goats.

Bring me one of them for my potion,
Otherwise you will suffer severe demotion,
This potion will cause poverty wipeout,
I also need eye of trout.'

The shining knight got the goat,
Ripped it out of the box from the dreadful boat,
It turned out that the eye of trout from Lake Kerrors,
Wiped out all these blood-curdling terrors.

Matthew Horder (9)
Pixmore Junior School, Letchworth

I Have An Allergy

I have an allergy, a pretty bad one too,
I'm allergic to my brother, whatever shall I do?
Whenever I'm near him, I have to explain,
Oh, my brother ain't half a pain!

I know I'm allergic cos there's this humungous itch,
Also my eye starts to twitch,
I go to the hospital to have tests,
I have to hide when we have guests.

Everyone says I'm an amazing creation,
I have to stay ten feet away when we go on vacation.
None of my friends seem to care,
By the way, writing this poem was just a dare.

Tamar Dulley (9)
Pixmore Junior School, Letchworth

Dolphins' Eyes

Stop making my home a black sea.
Why do you want to make me choke?
My home is the sea, but you make it hurt me.

Please stop this.
If we become extinct, us you will not miss.
So don't bother with a goodbye kiss,
Because us you won't miss.

Stop the pollution,
Unless you want to start a revolution!
Can't you find a way to stop?
If you don't you'll make us . . . *pop!*

Please show some love,
Unless you want us to go the skies up above.
Stop making our sea a black cloak,
Why do you want to make us choke?

My home is the sea,
But you make it hurt me.
My home is the sea,
But you make it hurt me.

Annie Summan (9)
Pixmore Junior School, Letchworth

About My Bubbling Budgies

Gracefully gliding through the air
Hiding - trying to get out there
Very loud I love them
So cute, people want to get them.

They are fluffy, you'd like them too
Funny when they jump on you
When you feed them, they sometimes chew
My grandad even feeds them stew.

Sometimes they go running away
They do it a lot, they did it today
Get silly and peck around
Acting like a circus clown.

They are fun, they make you jump
When they fly, you hear their wings thump
They're like a little bright star
Land on your fingers and think it's a bar.

Adam Fortune (9)
Pixmore Junior School, Letchworth

Sunflower

What being towers so high,
With its black face and bright yellow hair?
Like the sun, but it can't think,
Nor see, nor touch,
What amazing being is it?

Why are you so thin?
Your drooping head of fire and many arms,
Like a towering sea monster.
Your being defies belief.
As your day ends, many more grow and live,
Weird thing;
Your day will never end.

Luis Fernandes (7)
Pixmore Junior School, Letchworth

My Sunflower

A sunflower is yellow and bright
It is as bright as the sun.
It has sharp, rough leaves
And its black, round centre
Is as round as a plate.
It has a plain and fresh scent
Which smells like the countryside.

Elise Ceri Lambert (7)
Pixmore Junior School, Letchworth

Autumn

Autumn is cold and shivery.
It sounds like the sun is dying.
It feels like a shivering mountain.
It smells like rain from the sky.
It makes me feel very happy.
This is what autumn means to me.

Euan Ryan (7)
Pixmore Junior School, Letchworth

Autumn

Autumn is cold and freezing.
It sounds like the big waves crashing.
It looks like the huge trees are falling down.
It smells like boiling hot dogs.
It makes me feel very cold and slippery.

Kieran Shurmer-Elliott (7)
Pixmore Junior School, Letchworth

Autumn

Autumn is cold and damp.
It tastes like strong wind and fresh air.
It sounds like scattering leaves.
It looks like traffic lights.
It smells like dirt and mud.
It makes me feel like ice cream.

Kia Tarling (8)
Pixmore Junior School, Letchworth

Autumn

Autumn is cold, rainy and foggy.
It sounds like a wooden rain shaker when the trees blow.
It looks like a frozen, ice-cold fridge.
It smells like fresh water.
It makes me feel like I'm in a bath with ice.
That's autumn!

Scarlett Ross (8)
Pixmore Junior School, Letchworth

Autumn

Autumn is like all the brown leaves falling on me and it's cold.
It tastes like the wet, blue rain and the cold air.
It sounds like red leaves crunching and brown leaves falling off
the tree.
It smells like boiling soup.
It makes me feel relaxed.

Lauren Carter (7)
Pixmore Junior School, Letchworth

Cats

Some cats are good
Some cats are bad
Some cats are quite sad

Some cats are fat
Some cats are thin
Some cats like to hide in the garden bin

Some cats are slow
Some cats are fast
Some cats like to be last

Some cats are mean
Some cats are kind
Some cats like to use their mind.

Danielle Dulley (8)
Pixmore Junior School, Letchworth

Autumn

Autumn is cold and foggy.
It tastes like a cup of coffee or tea.
It sounds like rain pitter-pattering.
It looks like a bit of dark sky.
It smells like nature.
It makes me feel really, really happy!

Simon Kitching (7)
Pixmore Junior School, Letchworth

Autumn

Autumn is freezing like an iceberg and like ice cream.
It tastes like soup.
It sounds like rustling leaves.
It smells like bluebirds fluttering.
It looks like brown falling leaves.
It makes me feel like a freezing fridge.

Jared Guy (7)
Pixmore Junior School, Letchworth

Autumn

Autumn is fun and joyful.
It tastes like hot soup and warm vegetables.
It sounds like drifting wind in the cold air.
It looks like leaves drifting in the sky.
It smells like roses in the air.
It makes me feel happy, joyful and marvellous!

Claire-Amandine Sempala (7)
Pixmore Junior School, Letchworth

Autumn

I saw a brown conker in the afternoon.
Charlie came walking by
And we went to look for signs of autumn.
It looked like brown leaves falling off the trees.
It smelt like cut grass freshly mowed.
It tasted like chocolate cake.
It felt like crispy leaves.

Joseph Smith (7)
Pixmore Junior School, Letchworth

Autumn

Autumn is cold and crunchy.
It sounds like wings flapping.
It looks like an orange balloon.
It smells like hot chocolate.

Samuel West (7)
Pixmore Junior School, Letchworth

Autumn

Autumn is cold and crunchy.
It sounds like birds twittering.
It looks like colourful leaves.
It smells like hot tea and toast.
It makes me feel nice.

Sarah Jane Glatzhofer (7)
Pixmore Junior School, Letchworth

Autumn

Autumn is cold and slippery.
It sounds like naughty seagulls.
It looks like crabs hiding behind rocks.
It smells like smelly seaweed.

Chad Whitby (7)
Pixmore Junior School, Letchworth

Autumn

Autumn is cold and rainy.
It sounds like leaves falling.
It looks like rain flooding.
It smells like wood burning.
It feels like hot chocolate.

Ben Dulley (7)
Pixmore Junior School, Letchworth

Autumn

Autumn is crisp and cold.
It sounds like the wind blowing.
It looks like colourful snowflakes.
It smells like wood burning.

Jonathan Batt (7)
Pixmore Junior School, Letchworth

Autumn

Autumn is cold and nice.
It sounds like baby squirrels just born.
It looks like a carpet when the leaves fall from the trees.
It makes me feel calm inside.

Jessica Baines (7)
Pixmore Junior School, Letchworth

Autumn

It is autumn time.
The green leaves are turning to brown leaves that look like dirt.
I can hear the animals running away from the rain when it's raining.
It is very cold and we are starting to put on our raincoats.
The trees are waving in the breeze.

Kiera Brunton (7)
Pixmore Junior School, Letchworth

Autumn

Autumn is very brown.
When I walk through red and yellow,
I can hear crunches from the leaves.
The trees look bare and I feel very cold.
With the breeze blowing my hair,
It makes me feel like I'm in the middle of the wind.
This is how autumn makes me feel.

Leah Summan (8)
Pixmore Junior School, Letchworth

Autumn

Autumn is cold and the leaves are falling off trees.
You hear crunching when you step on a leaf.
They feel breakable when you touch them.
They sound like crunching and crackling sweet wrappers.
Autumn smells like cold and wet rain.
It tastes like freezing and frozen snow.
It looks like frosty and crackly hailstones.

Adam Carter (8)
Pixmore Junior School, Letchworth

Autumn

It is freezing cold in autumn.
When I go outside, the trees rustle like a river.
The water is cold.
Autumn tastes like a bowl of boiling soup.
The leaves have white, shining snow.
The snow is on the tree trunk.
The concrete becomes extremely slippery.
This is what I mean by autumn.

Ishan Loi (7)
Pixmore Junior School, Letchworth

Autumn

Autumn is cold and crisp.
It sounds like a squirrel scratching.
It looks like colourful snowflakes.
It smells like hot chocolate.

Terri Heeks (7)
Pixmore Junior School, Letchworth

Sunflower

Sunflowers are great
Sunflowers are tall
Sunflowers have windy, green leaves
Sunflowers are as golden as the summer sun
Sunflowers' petals are yellow and gold
Sunflowers' seeds are brown and yellow
Sunflowers have soft, yellow petals
Sunflowers' stalks are spiky and long
That is my best sunflower.

Tanisha-Marie Fountain (7)
Pixmore Junior School, Letchworth

Sunflower Poem

Lovely tall sunflower
Long green stem
As tall as a giraffe
As buttery as butter
Golden yellow petals
Lovely long sunflower
As yellow as custard.

Kimberley Clarke (7)
Pixmore Junior School, Letchworth

Sunflower

The sunflower is furry, like a kitten.
It sounds like the wind blowing it.
It looks like a sun in the bright sky.
It feels like your heart - a beautiful flower.
It smells like lavender.
It makes me feel like there is a rainbow in the sky.
A sunflower is so pretty.

Asharna Clark (7)
Pixmore Junior School, Letchworth

The Sunflower

As bright as the sun and Mars,
With a giant, prickly stem,
Poking through the clouds,
Always following the sun,
With giant green leaves,
Gleaming through the trees.
It's always smelling like honey,
It always surprises the bears,
Always makes me smile when I'm down,
Brightening the day with its golden petals.
It's a *sunflower!*

Grace Twitchett (7)
Pixmore Junior School, Letchworth

Sunflower

The sunflower is as bright as the sun.
It smells as sweet as honey
And has glorious, golden, glittering petals around its head
With seeds in the middle.
Sunflowers are the best and they make me happy.

Lewis White (7)
Pixmore Junior School, Letchworth

The Sunflower

As bright as the sun,
The head of the flower is as round as a bun.
The stem is as spiky as a porcupine,
Sunflowers love their talkie time.
They have giant green leaves
And sunflowers live near the trees.
Sunflowers are my favourite flowers.

Ruth Fox (7)
Pixmore Junior School, Letchworth

Autumn

Autumn is when leaves are falling off the trees.
It tastes like delicious stew on the BBQ.
It sounds like leaves scratching together.
It looks like brown leaves in drifts.
It smells like a conker tree with conkers popping.
It makes me feel jolly and happy.
That's autumn.

Aislinn Rainey (7)
Pixmore Junior School, Letchworth

Autumn

Autumn is when leaves float down from the trees.
It tastes like hot dogs.
It sounds like leaves rustling.
It looks like leaves falling from the trees.
It smells like a barbecue.
It makes me feel chilly.
That's autumn.

Akshay Dhunna (7)
Pixmore Junior School, Letchworth

Autumn

Autumn is golden yellow and bright orange.
It looks like leaves waving.
It sounds like leaves swooshing to the ground.
It looks like trees wailing.
It smells like hot chocolate.
It makes me feel happy.

Gerardo Esposito (7)
Pixmore Junior School, Letchworth

Autumn

Autumn is golden yellow and bright orange.
It sounds like trees swaying from side to side.
It looks like a big cosy blanket.
It smells like hot dogs and burgers.

Joseph Hathway-Neville (7)
Pixmore Junior School, Letchworth

Rabbits

Some rabbits are fluffy
Some rabbits are not
Some rabbits have lots and lots of spots

Some rabbits are black
Some rabbits are white
Some rabbits go out of our sight

Some rabbits are fat
Some rabbits are thin
Some rabbits jump into the bin

Some rabbits are short
Some rabbits are tall
But I like rabbits - all.

Kerry Davis (8)
Pixmore Junior School, Letchworth

Autumn

Autumn is yellow and rainy.
It tastes like sweet sugar.
It sounds like the windy breeze.
It looks like sunny butter.
It smells like smelly trees.
It makes me feel super happy.
That's autumn!

Bradley Baynes (8)
Pixmore Junior School, Letchworth

Autumn

Autumn is golden yellow and chocolate-brown.
It sounds like hedgehogs sniffing through the crunching leaves.
It looks like a warm blanket touching the ground.
It smells like chocolate and hot dogs.

Rhys Jackson (7)
Pixmore Junior School, Letchworth

Autumn

Autumn is golden brown and bright yellow leaves.
It tastes like hot chocolate and biscuits.
It sounds like animals running to hibernate.
It looks like leaves falling on the grey pavement.
It smells like marshmallows.
It makes me feel cosy.
That's autumn.

Florence Gorski-Giles (7)
Pixmore Junior School, Letchworth

Autumn

Autumn is cold and crispy.
It tastes like milk chocolate cookies.
It sounds like children playing in the leaves.
It looks like small bits of paint on a piece of paper.
It smells like the gas from the fireworks.
It makes me feel cold.

Charlie Bohm (7)
Pixmore Junior School, Letchworth

Autumn

Autumn is red and green with yellow.
It tastes like sausage rolls and hot chocolate.
It sounds like crackling leaves on the hard concrete.
It looks like bare trees and the wind carrying them.
It smells like snow falling.
It feels like coal on the fire.

Darnell Jackson (7)
Pixmore Junior School, Letchworth

Snowy, Snowy

Snowy, Snowy smooth and soft
Doesn't live up in a loft,
As she munches carrots and corn
She is glad that she was born.

Snowy, Snowy munch, crunch, munch
She has lettuce for her lunch,
She likes hiding in dark places
Snowy, Snowy, squeak, squeak, squeak.

Snowy, Snowy squeaky sound
Scampers fast around the hutch,
Clutches hold of a carrot
And eats it all, munch, munch, munch.

Ruth Bainbridge (9)
Pixmore Junior School, Letchworth

Kitten, Kitten

Kitten, kitten safe and snug,
Under a comfortable rug.
Rolling, running, leaping high,
Jumping till she touched the sky.

Kitten, kitten tabby fur,
Oh, I love to hear you purr.
You have very lovely paws,
But you have very, very sharp claws.

Kitten, kitten on the floor,
Lying right next to the door.
Playing with her lovely toys,
She can make a lot of noise.

Kitten, kitten you're the best,
Sometimes you can be a pest.
Sleeping cosy in your bed,
Lifting up your gentle head.

Sophie Jones (9)
Pixmore Junior School, Letchworth

Monkey, Monkey

Monkey, monkey in a tree,
Eating fruit, so leave it be.
They can be very cheeky,
But also a bit freaky.

Monkey, monkey go and play,
Go have some fun through the day.
Then go have a little rest,
Oh, monkey you are the best.

Monkey, monkey ooh-ooh-ah!
You are not a predator.
Fur soft as a lion's mane
And can sometimes be a pain.

Monkey, monkey swing so high,
Like they are trying to fly.
Eyes so delicate and bright,
They sometimes give you a fright.

Monkey, monkey soft and shy,
Oh, monkey you swing so high.
Silly monkey, you can't fly,
Go on monkey, say goodbye!

Megan Keighley (10)
Pixmore Junior School, Letchworth

Tiger, Tiger

Tiger, tiger snow-white fur,
He's a cat but he doesn't purr!
Pitch-black stripes like marker pen,
Legs thicker than old Big Ben.

Tiger, tiger in the sun,
On a rock and having fun.
Eating antelope all day,
Always having time to play.

Tiger, tiger razor claws,
Always breaking animal laws.
Running, running for its prey,
Chewing, chewing as it lays.

Tiger, tiger glistening eyes,
Listens to animal cries.
Sleeping in the hot warm sun,
End of day but has had fun.

Malachi Lalite (9)
Pixmore Junior School, Letchworth

Fish

Some fish are fat
Some fish are slim
All fish love to swim, swim, swim

Some fish are coloured
Some fish are plain
Some fish get put down the drain

Some fish are fast
Some fish are slow
Some fish just grow and grow and grow

Some fish are old
Some fish are young
Some fish even have a tongue.

Jack Horder (8)
Pixmore Junior School, Letchworth

Rats

Some rats are good
Some rats are bad
Some rats get rabies and go all mad

Some rats are brown
Some rats are black
Some rats get chased by all sorts of cats

Some rats are fat
Some rats are thin
Some rats like to eat out of the bin

Some rats are short
Some rats are tall
But I don't like rats, not at all!

Thomas Bunyan (9)
Pixmore Junior School, Letchworth

If I Could Change The World

When I rule the universe,
There will be no school,
No sprouts,
No broccoli or cabbage,
Cool!
When I rule the universe.

When I rule the universe,
The sun will shine all day and night,
Except,
In winter,
When thick snow will be bright.
When I rule the universe.

Annabelle Schofield (11)
St Thomas More Middle School, Norwich

Would You Like To Be . . .

Would you like to be a shopkeeper,
Sitting in a shop all day,
Or a customer there to pay
For the food, maybe a toy,
For your child - a little girl or boy?

Would you like to be a nurse,
In a surgery looking at blood,
Or rather helping after a tsunami or flood,
Feeding the old and curing the new,
Knowing they're happy to finally be safe with you?

Mollie Armes (11)
St Thomas More Middle School, Norwich

When I Grow Up

When I grow up I want to be a singer/songwriter,
Doing my favourite things,
Singing and writing non-stop,
Flashing a load of gold rings.

I'd have my own dressing room,
With my name engraved on a star,
I'd sing in London and Paris,
And travel in a sleek, white limo car.

I'd sail to many countries
And take over the stage,
I'd be bigger than Britney Spears,
Until I reach a very old age.

I'd be best friends with Jojo,
I'd dine out to dinner with Sting,
I'd grab a microphone and my limo,
Whenever I felt the urge to sing.

I'd invent all the best dance moves,
My songs would be the latest choice,
My CDs would be completely awesome
And my band would be called *Voice*.

I'd live in the grandest of mansions,
The bath would be made out of gold,
But that's going to be a long time from now,
Because I'm only nine years old.

Rowan Perrow (9)
St Thomas More Middle School, Norwich

If I Could Change The World

If I could change the world,
There would be no more stress,
No wars, no dying, no killing forever,
It would be a world of happiness and love,
If I could change the world.

If I could change the world,
There would be no more school,
No more hassle, no rush, no getting told off,
It would be a world of peace and fun.

If I could change the world,
There would be no more anger,
No slaps, no stomps, no tears of fear,
It would be a world of safety and love.

If I could change the world,
There would be no more splits,
No breaks, no sadness, no arguments,
It would be a world of happiness and family,
A world in which joy and love would grow,
If I could change the world.

Cleo Anderson (11)
St Thomas More Middle School, Norwich

Would You Want To Be A Leader Of Men?

Would you want to be a leader of men?
Tell them off, do as you please,
Boss them about and they will do as you say,
They will fight people who bully you.

Would you want to be a leader of men?
Be admired and loved everywhere,
But sometimes you can be let down
By their immature, childish and sluggish behaviour.

Would you want to be a leader of men?
Be insulted by their slang use of language,
Be disgusted by their obsession of football,
But if there were no men, you wouldn't exist!

Lucy Zhuang (10)
St Thomas More Middle School, Norwich

If I Could Change The World

If I could change the world,
I would make it much more fair,
If I could change the world,
Everyone would share.

If I could change the world,
Hatred would be love,
If I could change the world,
Nobody would shove.

If I could change the world,
Everyone would be nice.
     Definitely!

Caroline Fleet (11)
St Thomas More Middle School, Norwich

When I Grow Up . . .

When I grow up I want to be an author,
Writing for people's delight,
I want to write fantasy stories,
Getting them transported to shops every night.

When I grow up I want to be a singer
And have a very good band,
With loads of screaming fans chasing me,
Travel in a cool, hippy van.

When I grow up I want to be a film star,
Earning loads of cash,
Having a glamorous lifestyle
And eating sausages and mash.

When I grow up I want to be an artist,
Painting beautiful pictures,
Drawing and colouring would be bliss
And giving university art lectures.

Ciara Clark (9)
St Thomas More Middle School, Norwich

If I Could Change The World

If I could change the world,
There would be no more harmful drugs,
No more cigarettes,
If I could change the world,
No one would be allowed to paint post boxes different colours,
People would always love their children,
No more care homes for the old,
If I could change the world.

Danielle Begley (8)
St Thomas More Middle School, Norwich

If I Could Change The World

If I could change the world,
I'd close down all the schools
And instead of doing work,
We'd swim in swimming pools.

If I could change the world,
Nobody would die,
Because it would be wonderful
And people would be able to fly.

If I could change the world,
I'd make dreams come true,
I'd make the world so brilliant,
No one would feel blue.

Euan Douglas (9)
St Thomas More Middle School, Norwich

When I Grow Up

When I grow up I want to be a comedian,
I want everyone to laugh at me,
I want to be the best of the best,
I want to be better than the rest,
I want money,
Life to be sunny,
I want to be a joker,
Have a great hand at poker,
When I grow up.

Jordan Baker (10)
St Thomas More Middle School, Norwich

When I Grow Up

When I grow up I want to be a psychologist,
I will make people feel good,
I will help them through hard parts of their lives,
I will make them feel sane like they should,
I will tell them to feel confident,
I will make them feel that succeed at their endeavours they could.

When I grow up I will be a psychologist,
I will make people feel happy,
I will put them in a long, white chair,
They will confess their deepest fears to me,
I will make them feel it's alright,
I will make them content, hopefully.

When I grow up I will be a psychologist,
Well, I'm not that sure, actually.

Joseph Robson (10)
St Thomas More Middle School, Norwich

When I Grow Up

When I grow up I want to travel the world,
Find new, exotic places,
Find animals that haven't been discovered,
Feed and save wonderful and weird creatures.

When I grow up I want to be a famous pop star,
Who everyone loves,
I want to go on lots of tours,
Be on the front cover of every magazine and newspaper.

When I grow up I want to learn witchcraft,
Put spells on people,
Not allow anyone to die,
Fly up in the sky.

Florence Horspole (9)
St Thomas More Middle School, Norwich

If I Were An Animal . . .

If I were an animal,
I'd be a penguin,
It's a fun life, nothing can kill me,
When I'm gliding through the sea and ice.

Charles Escott (9)
St Thomas More Middle School, Norwich